Dedicated to those with a lifelong commitment to ethical principles.

M.D. Tophus

The Psychological Impacts of Labelling and Failure to Diagnose.

Hilphma Publications 2022. www.hilphmapublication.com

First Edition.

Germany.

The author has over 25 years of clinical experience in the healthcare field. Is cognisant of both DSM-5-TR (and previous versions) and ICD-11 (and previous versions) disorders and conditions; quality and safety improvement in healthcare; and healthcare education

Other M.D. Tophus publications available:

"Exercising Quality in Healthcare Service Provision: A Complex Care Workbook for All Healthcare Professionals." Germany: Hilphma Publications: 2022.

"Who is This Colleague?: Dangers of the Healthcare Profession, and beyond. An Interview Guide for Recruitment, Performance Appraisal and Post-Adverse Events."
Germany: Hilphma Publications: 2022.

"Think on your Feet: Those Who Can. For the Consummate Healthcare Professional."
Germany: Hilphma Publications: 2022.

"The Unfortunate Healthcare Treater, The Hapless Healthcare Therapist: Narcissistic and Borderline Personality Disorder clients. The Grit."
Germany: Hilphma Publications: 2022.

"Victims of Crime: Introduction to Forensic Challenges in Healthcare."
Germany: Hilphma Publications: 2022.

"The A to Z of Workplace Bullying: For the Healthcare Professional and Beyond."
Germany: Hilphma Publications: 2022.

"Trauma United, Life Defined. A Healthcare Tool for Professionals Across the Globe."
Germany: Hilphma Publications: 2022.

"Reflective Thinking: the True Healthcare Tool."
Germany: Hilphma Publications: 2022.

"Burnout in Healthcare"
Germany: Hilphma Publications: 2022.

"Reasonable Resilience in Workplaces and Healthcare Work"
Germany: Hilphma Publications: 2022.

CONTENTS

Slander, libel and defamation are principal concepts which come to mind in the event of labelling of an individual.

Labelled victims are of all shapes, sizes, ages, cultures and beliefs. From a variety of backgrounds and socio-economic groups.

The psychology of labelling does not just involve the impact upon the victim but conversely serves a psychological purpose for the labeller/s.

The derivation of enjoyment, pleasure, projection of anger, jealousy, rage, inadequacy and inherent bullying mentality, is at the core of the labeller's modus operandi.

Professionals, students, and many other categories can seek to, and indeed, initiate labelling behaviors.

It can also be derived from frustration in not penetrating the core of the labelled individual. The misplaced angst involved in misunderstanding a person, the labelled person refusing to conform or relent, or place on display elements of their inner being, with different choices made regarding career, socialisation, the way of seeing the world, choice of extra-curricular activities undertaken and differing socio-politico- cultural views held, all can predispose a vulnerable person to the process of labelling.

Once labelling is perpetrated in written form, the victim often has minimal recourse (unless they access effective resources, or have the capacity and means to pursue legal action).

Failure to diagnose (as in the title of this publication) is used in several contextual meanings.

Firstly that, where the labeller's intents, plans and actions are misunderstood comes the misdiagnosis of the core problem and therefore a substantial problem in preventing further labelling and defamation.

Secondly, failure to diagnose, or misdiagnose, the seriousness of the pending slander and libel- and is often passed off as recalcitrant or juvenile behaviors which will soon relent prior to labelling, moving towards more deleterious paths.

Thirdly, as exemplification of issues faced by some patients in healthcare environments- that of failure to diagnose, and the consequences which can prevail post-haste.

Thus, this resource provides a challenge to the reader to diagnose effectively.

In the case of healthcare, for instance, where a patient is wrongly/incorrectly labelled as a 'trouble-maker' or worse, 'mad', then the documentation is often passed to other treaters- predisposing the labelled patient to each treater believing that the label is the 'truth', regardless of whether it has been initially written by one single treater, alone.

M.D. Tophus publication 'Victims of Crime: Introduction to Forensic Challenges in Healthcare.' has particular cross-relevance to this current resource (1)

Thus, this publication provides comprehensive exploration of labelling, from: defamation (slander and libel); derivation of enjoyment (schadenfreude, projected blame, incentivised hatred, addictive vilification, and multiple other categories) through to ethical healthcare and patient effects.
The failure to diagnose the reasons and impacts of labelling is examined on 3 primary levels. Questions are provided for further clarification of the information provided.

<u>DEFAMATION</u>

Please note, that some of the content featured below is country and State dependant, and may vary dependant upon the country in which the defamation occurs/occurred. The information provided is general in nature, only.

<u>Defamation definition:</u>

Act/s of reputational damage to an individual, or group, by way of false written or oral statements provided to a third party presented as factual.

<u>Defamation summary:</u>

-there are 2 distinct categories: slander (oral defamation); and, libel (written defamation)

-defamation can also involve paintings, photographs, drawings and the making of physical gestures

-re-tweeting also constitutes defamation (spreading the word)

-for law suits (dependant upon the country) one must prove actual harm, for instance- mental anguish

-impacts: dismissal from job; loss of business; direct stress-induced physical injury problem/s; loss of status (for instance, shunned by work colleagues, family or friends); ostracization from community/ies, reputational damage

-'Defamation per se': can involve, job impact: wrongly claimed inability to undertake work effectively or purporting to be morally corrupt/lacking integrity to undertake work tasks

-seeking of damages: punitive; economic; and non-economic damages, categories

Defamation examples

False accusations of: misconduct, criminality (theft, assault for instance), infidelity, lying about professional accreditations.

Defamation definition relevant to healthcare

"False statements about an employee which can either be written, oral, or naturally both, is defamation at its basis.
That is, libel, and slander, respectively.
The impact: damage to patient referrals; loss of revenue; and, loss of job.
To illustrate: colleague spreads false rumours about a healthcare worker; or, negative reviews on social media sites, and numerous other modes." (2)

Defamation in healthcare environments

Much has been written about defamation suffered by healthcare workers. Little, however, has been examined about the affects of defamation on patients in private and public healthcare environments.

This can involve a patient challenging a healthcare provider's clinical incompetence or falsified statements.

To exemplify:

-false statements (medication misuse, or illicit undertakings regarding medication), irresponsibility in dealing with health condition/s; incorrect mentally ill or factitious disorder labelling;

-negligent statements (in for example medical records); defamation of character upon (for instance) life choices, lifestyle grounds;

-slanderous or libelous statements made about a patient who also works in healthcare (as a response to whistleblowing, for eg) which affects work status, workload, or business activity;

-threatening a patient that if they make a complaint against the doctor, or healthcare unit, that they will suffer consequences and threatening to weaponise litigation against the patient for any formal complaint made

Claiming doctor-patient confidentiality/privilege regarding subpoena of notes may not apply.

For the healthcare worker, the issue of defamatory job references with false statements, though must prove malicious intent, applies to this category. This can either be slanderous, or libelous, in nature.

-Targets: whistleblowers, researchers, academics etc

-Mode: whistleblowing against (eg public) officials, groups and individuals who are involved in misconduct, corruption, human rights abuses (against individuals or groups)

-SLAPP threats: used as prevention, silencing, harrassment, intimidation, gagging and deterrence of whistleblowing or reporting (above, or similar issues) are common in USA, UK and Europe.

Defamation as specific to 1 healthcare environment

-A healthcare worker in an emergency hospital unit is required to urgently insert a urinary catheter after a failed attempt by a community healthcare worker (resulting in the patient's blood loss and injury).

-The healthcare worker is also part of a clinical response team who later reports a doctor for negligence and professional misconduct (involving the same patient).

-The patient involved later dies in the same hospital.

-The reported doctor becomes aggressively defamatory, making untrue and damaging accusations about the clinician.

-The clinical worker suffers significant stress, anxiety, and concurrent physical ailments.

-They are thence rendered unable to function at work.

Defamation as specific to 1 specialisation in healthcare

-An individual reports corruption involving a large organization.

 -Is hospitalised following police involvement, psychiatric involvement and threat of scheduling as a result.

Defamation and patient safety

-A general practitioner falsifies his medical records in response to a subpoena for a patient's notes.

-The falsified medical records are then passed on to the patient's newly appointed general practitioner resulting in dangerous effects (life-threatening) upon the patient's treatment.

Defamation and mediation

-mediation is commonly referred to as one form of 'alternative dispute resolution' (dependant upon the country). Mediation processes are pertinent to both civil and criminal defamation

-mediator: is considered a neutral third party

-mediation is similar to 'negotiation' (they both use a neutral third party), and is likewise non-legally binding

-'arbitration' (on the other hand) is legally binding and mutually enforceable.

Defamation and court processes

With relevance, is the UK defamation act 1996; 2013. The 2013 act includes social media (includes re-tweets); is considered permanent in form; and, causes serious damage to reputation.

In Australia: where there is proof of publication of defamation, in this case you do not need to further substantiate it.

This includes, for example, Facebook statements though there are state by state differences.

Factors involved:
One person or more reads the defamatory comment; identifiable victim or their business; is defamatory- the average person reading it would be lead to think less of the defamed person; can cause serious harm; and, is indefensible.
There is a 1 year limitation period in Australia (from first defamatory comment).
Libel is described as a permanent form of communication defamation style.

In Germany, the 'general right of personality' exists in regards to defamation, and other similar cases (like privacy violations). The law even covers protection of a deceased person's relatives under the 'general right of personality'.

Examples include:

-accusations of sub-standard or negligent care made by fellow staff or managers with falsification of patient records to back the claim, and justification of job dismissal of the individual healthcare worker

-retaliation against staff members (eg agency staff not usually part of
the clinical unit) via false statements about performance involving non-adherence to patient safety.

-if an employer does not publish/forward a defamatory statement (false statement of fact) about an employee to a third party, then they may not be libel

-many factors are at play: but to use the example of defamation based psychological suffering, anxiety and distress precluding one from immediate return to work (following dismissal of the employer/offending party), the following applies: diagnostic- psychological suffering- points system (level of distress determined via psychiatric or psychological assessment processes); recommendations made for workplace (or external) rehabilitation counselling scheme and formulated rehabilitation program; often lengthy time off work; progressive return to full time work; limited duties/work tasks initially; feedback mechanisms to rehabilitation advisor and employer; workplace performance review, and sign off; and, ideally- prevention of recurrence of bullying, labelling, or further defamatory statements.

Defamation and protections

-if you have been defamed by a work colleague, and your employer refuses to file a worker's compensation claim (due to your resultant injury), this becomes an issue of legality for the employer

-generally, one is protected by worker's compensation laws

-following legal advice one may report a work colleague (for instance) to upper management to initiate conduct reviews, and preventative measures from further defamatory comments and/or statements

-mediation, and alternative dispute resolution, processes may be pursued

-alternative work arrangements (workplace environment changes, removal of offending work colleague, new contractual agreements, work from home).

Defamation and individual perpetrator types

Some generalised individual perpetrator types include:

-vengeful;

-compulsive liars;

-attention-seekers;

-projected guilt(y);

-secondary agenda based;

-disclosed malingerers;

-radical group affiliates;

-enduring hate mongerers;

-defamers who fear being defamed.

<u>SLANDER</u>

The M.D. Tophus publication 'The A to Z of Workplace Bullying: For the
Healthcare Professional and Beyond' (2) is particularly pertinent to these defamation
based topics.

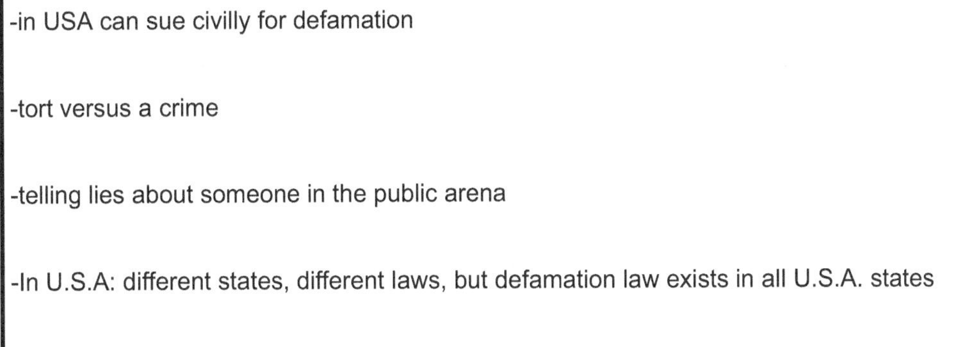

Slander definition:

-spoken defamation

-false statement of fact- damage to reputation or character

-in USA can sue civilly for defamation

-tort versus a crime

-telling lies about someone in the public arena

-In U.S.A: different states, different laws, but defamation law exists in all U.S.A. states

-results in economic harm to victim or loss to business, psychological suffering, and so
 forth.

Slander definition, relevant to healthcare environments

"This is essentially, spoken defamation.
In illustration: harmful speech about job performance; application of clinical practice; and,
communication style.
Personality; and mental acuity, is additionally integrative.
Capacity to continue working (affecting number of referrals; and practice as a whole), is
ultimately at issue." (2)

-As indicated above, slander is defamation in the transient form (eg spoken word)

-some are 'actionable per se': not necessary to prove.

This includes false accusations regarding committing of a crime (incarcerable crime), professional misconduct or incapability, or having a contagious disease.

There are two primary categories of slander:

-Slander per se

-Slander (not 'slander per se'): have to prove special damages.

Factors:

-false statement of fact--> made to a third party--> damage to reputation of the slandered --> proof of negligent behavior (ie slanderer did not check whether the statement was true or false before making the statement)--> made via malice or reckless disregard--> private individuals: reasonable person not make the statement.

LIBEL

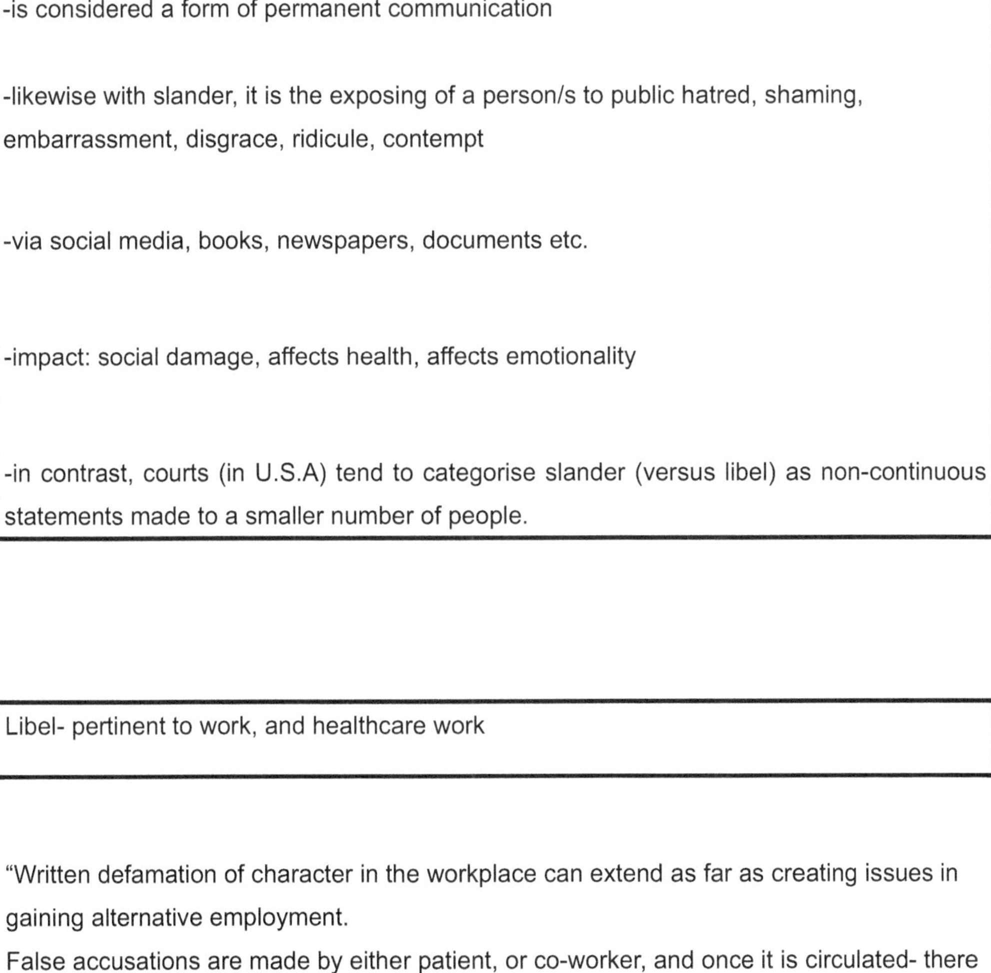

Libel definition:

-written defamation

-is considered a form of permanent communication

-likewise with slander, it is the exposing of a person/s to public hatred, shaming, embarrassment, disgrace, ridicule, contempt

-via social media, books, newspapers, documents etc.

-impact: social damage, affects health, affects emotionality

-in contrast, courts (in U.S.A) tend to categorise slander (versus libel) as non-continuous statements made to a smaller number of people.

Libel- pertinent to work, and healthcare work

"Written defamation of character in the workplace can extend as far as creating issues in gaining alternative employment.
False accusations are made by either patient, or co-worker, and once it is circulated- there is an inherent problem, to say the least.
The false accusations can promote other forms of vilification toward the libelled.
Legal representation is a given." (2)

There are two main categories of libel:

-Libel, and

-Libel per se: e.g. false statements about committing of a crime, sexual misconduct or impropriety, or improper professional conduct

 - in print, or on the internet (eg reviews)

 -social media- lies, false rumours

-results in economic harm to victim or loss to business, psychological suffering.

Libel and healthcare- written reviews

-in several countries, there exists laws, and website, disclaimers (social media platforms' protection from liability) from doctors being able to sue for bad reviews

-anonymity of many reviewers mean that doctors cannot provide the proof of author required to bring about a lawsuit (but 'john doe' suits, if proof of a defamation case, then one may acquire a subpoena to trace the internet protocol details of the reviewer).

The DERIVATION of ENJOYMENT

It is a sad state of affairs when one realises that there are many individuals who derive pleasure from another person's suffering, and furthermore, are willing to initiate and continuously perpetrate upon the target until they 'break', or appear 'broken'.

Each individual, across the world, has the inner capacity to undertake such plans, injurious words, degrading actions, and unforgivable behaviors, of this type. However, each make their choice to enact, or to take the higher ground. It is a relief to know that a great number of persons make the latter choice, regardless of the ease involved in just 'going with the group'.

Nevertheless, one must focus on those who indeed choose a different path altogether. The vehicle by which they undertake these deleterious behaviors is not necessarily due to enacting their own hurts, discomforts, madness, aggression, or indoctrinated desire for toxicity.

It can, however, emerge from some of the reasons below, and likewise be executed so forth:

the 'how':

-expectations of masochistic acceptance from the victim

-righteousness, entitlement

-sect-like adherence

-guided by unscrupulous leaders

-sensationalism of private individuals, replicating that which is modelled in for e.g., social
 media

-pessimistic personification and anti-adulation based behaviors

-this differs from 'schadenfreude', as schadenfreude is a passive form (that is, the malicious pleasure is derived from circumstances- already created plight- for the victim, as opposed to actively bringing about the target's losses, or misery).

the 'why':

-sadism and sexualised pleasure from another's suffering

-sectarianism

-hatred for no reason, projected hatred away from oneself, hate because of false beliefs about the target

-victim's perceived non-conformity, and non-compliance

-bringing about change for entertainment value

-grandiose delusions

-identification with the debauched

-criminal connections, criminality

-co-dependant personality types

-sociopathy, and psychopathy

-nouveau creationism

-pecking order

-survival of the fittest

-purely that monstrous behaviors breed contempt and resultant content (pleasure)

-perverse incentivisations: notoriety, notability, grandiosity, group acceptance, external
  reward

-perceive the victim as deserving of suffering, and nothing more

-to humiliate

-to embarrass

-to create enduring angst, physical and psychological suffering of the victim.

and, the 'how and why'

-salaciousness (salivating perversity) borne of rumour, innuendo, and dangerous gossip

-frenzied, insatiable behaviors which are triggered by promise of ongoing
  exotic lies and deceit

-new rule of law

-power in numbers creates acceptability of askewed quasi philosophical bents

-grandstanding as a form of reassuring oneself of one's existence.

Of course, there can be many other factors at play- including gaslighting, which are featured above and below in this publication.

There are multiple understandings of outright labelling and targetting to be examined- upon which require extrapolation.

Several categories exist, such as:

SCHADENFREUDE

Schadenfreude definition:

Enjoyment at observing or being aware of another person/s experiencing of misfortune.

Multiple cultures have a word synonymous with the meaning of schadenfreude.

This is not to contradict the statement earlier regarding the passivity of schadenfreude. However, once a miserable circumstance (for instance) takes hold upon an individual, schadenfreude can become both the modus operandi and encircle the victim with that persona.

Following experiencing feelings of schadenfreude, unscrupulous other individuals (in group form, or otherwise) take full advantage of the situation and further the misery for the target. Thus, from passive to active indomitable actions.

Via, for example:

-earned, 'deserving of victimisation': rivalry and hatred

-jealousy

-helps further a cause of the group

-personalised projection, enjoyment for one's own pleasure to elevate self or for conceptualised self-betterment, or to increase perpetrators' self-esteem

-competition via group, or quintain like individual, rejection

-social desirability

-manipulation of victim to lower status

-the opposite to empathising with the target, derivation of enjoyment at suffering is core in-group versus out-group justification

-enhancement of schadenfreude via group solidarity

-in work based situations, can be exemplified via upper management versus employee

therefore, a source of both justification and pleasure for the perpetrators- combined.

PERVERSION:

how one derives eroticised pleasure from another's misery, derogation, reception of hatred, and seeks to satisfy cravings by instigating more misery. Reasons include:

-insatiable craving only satisfied by the success of misery making

-loving feelings are replaced by perversity of thought, action and word

-enjoyment of exercising wrong versus right

-urgent need to place into realisation an inherent lack of empathy

-'breaking the rules' as content of character.

Aim for victims' REJECTION FROM SOCIETY:

-enduring competitive pursuit

-group domination (in-group)

-reinforcement of social cohesion by focus upon a rejected individual/group prey

-sentimental hark back to classic schoolyard bullying

-re-affirmation of target as pathetic, uninteresting, a throw away

-thorough expectation that the earmarked person will accept her/his 'lot'

-incessant infliction of humiliation, isolation and exclusion.

<u>***PERCEIVED DEVIANCE, of victim:***</u>

<u>***-deviance primary, and secondary, in labelling***</u>

-all consuming concept of criminality/criminal mind of the 'labelled individual'
(via judging others by own standards, and guilt- even where there is an incapability of guilt,
or remorseful feelings, are present)

-false accusations of the victim having committed a crime become more and more
enhanced, and stories altered

-judging others by one's own untitled deviancy

-utilisation of 'bait and switch' regarding another's true life story

-example: when a relative attempts to save a family member from certain death, and is
then slandered, libelled and labelled as having undertaken the exact opposite.

<u>**REHABILITATE to 'NORMAL'**</u>

<u>**Concept: you are not me, therefore I cannot relate to you, thus you must be rehabilitated to the 'normal'**</u>

-normal: the definition of the word, in this sense, is: conforming to an accepted standard which is expected or typical.

-relate: is defined as: create or display a connection between; identification with

-rehabilitated (in this vein): is understood to be defined as, to: reintegrate by facilitating toward the accepted standard of thought, behavior, and actions, often by progressive reward.

Alternatively: restoration to normal life or health via education, or therapeutic measures- following incarceration, sickness or addiction.

identification of different elements of culture and heritage

-integrates many different factors (covered above, and below).

<u>*INVESTED ALLEGIANCE (of perpetrators):*</u>

-self-identity focus

-perverse incentivisations

-payments

-rewards (intrinsic and extrinsic)

-accreditations

-social credit

-furthering explicit and implicit biases

-life-long membership within a group

-labelling to increase hierarchical greatness.

RELIGIOSITY:

This explanation, naturally, does not pertain to all with religious/ spiritual beliefs.

-for the good of the target

-make the marked individual hit rock bottom they will see the light

-debase; deride; criticise every move, action, word; reduce to tears; segregate; isolate; annihilate; humiliate; ascetic humour; outcast; terminate as an individual

-superiority in religion/religious groups, thus inferiority of the victim

-extends to professional pursuits;

-malice and hatred are not being undertaken when it is in the 'name of god'

-spreading false rumours; singling out for ridicule; promoted to group as enjoyable for all ages

-targetting is okay because others do it

-vehicle to apprehend the target's sense of being; beyond pontification

-targetting is okay because we pray to a higher power, we are not bad

-in and out group

-us and them promoted as a concept ad infinitem

-a form of socialism

see 'socialism' category for expansion upon

-quoting theology, proverbs, or texts to back up targetting

-without exemplifying known theological texts which are commonly utilised, and often
(in cases of targetting) weaponised, the following generalised and extemporised
concepts are relevant

-schadenfreude as a point of meaningful reflection for closer relationship with a higher
power

see 'schadenfreude' category for more

-blind disgust at the 'out' group individual

-nil reference to chosen lifestyles, where appropriate, this pertains solely to not being an accepted part of the in-group

-projected rejection based on historical personal experiences

-apparent historically suffered (by the perpetrator'/s') sleights, sensitivities, misgivings, insecurities, idiosyncracies, mannerisms, misspoken words, culminate to either lack of empathy, indifference or vengefulness projected, promoted and justified by the perpetrator/s

-blind belief, no reasoning with, this is 'the way'

-difference breeds necessary contempt

-go with the groups' actions and thinking or become prey oneself

-perceived necessity to target

-targetting the individual as demonstrative of internal and external affiliations with political movements to increase group membership, funding, achieve higher status, and recruit otherwise unlikely members. For the sake of appearing modernised (for recruitment, tithing, other similar purposes, and to compete with new age religious movements) embracing the politics of the day (eg extremist climate change agendas).

-Incentivisation; reward (guaranteed entry into the after life; or gaining blessed worldly goods during lifetime)

-verbal abuse, and physical violence, as justifiable force or punishment of difference

-key words; code words; name calling; derision via group camaraderie targetting; punching inanimate objects (eg fence between properties) which represent difference, a target's rights

-lifestyle differences are fairgame (eg woman alone, unmarried, no children, considered part of a minority, from a different culture, not born in the neighborhood or country)

-the target's refusal to adopt the same lifestyle behaviors (puritanism) ensures ongoing vilification

-as the object of their obsession continues to resist- an attempt to hold their head up (to overcome the torment)- the group/individual representative of the group weaponises puritanism becoming more and more puritanical, so that every thing the victim does is wrong, evil, and punishable.

SOCIALISM:

-*Utopianism* (and modern version of utopian socialism): under the guise of moral equality is at its essence

-typically, idealism by which a perfect society and community can be achieved

-some members believe that this has already been achieved

-the definition of perfection in society is not of purist form, take for example the desire for a perfect society whereby criminals remain unpunished and police presence is anathema

-*Anarchism* (and collective anarchism): anti-institutionalism, anti-authority, anti-capitalism, and anti-government

-the latter (Collective Anarchism): anti-state and post-revolutionary

-*Communism* (extreme socialism, and anarcho-communism): anti-capitalism, anti-individualism, anti-private property ownership, working together for the common good, free consumption for all. Goal: (socially) classless society

-Anarcho-communism is similar to collective anarchism

-*Communitarianism:* primary belief is that an individual's personality and identity (socially) is formed and evolved via community interactivity

-*Radicalism:* which is often synonymous with fanaticism involves rejection of other points of view; is pro-change via extreme measures to alter current social systems

-Nihilism and Revolutionism are two of several styles of radicalism

This (as with many other ideologies) means that members do not take no for an answer, reject the core philosophy underlying individualism, and demand compliance at all costs.

The psychology of the (deviant) socialist thinker- what binds all of the above, is: the use of socially aggressive tactics to achieve the members' aims

-targetting of individuals is 'the norm', a means to achieve their end

-these non-negotiable behaviors ultimately cause the targetted individual (or group) no end of suffering.

<u>***COMMUNALIST and SOCIALISTIC THINKING:***</u>

-ethno-centric (former term)

-primary divisions enhanced between faiths, religions, ethnicities, concepts and beliefs

-individualism is the anti...

-group leaders decide: behaviors, beliefs, actions and outer individual/group targets
 in a communal way

-sense of cohesion, camaraderie, bonding, and pledges (is at its core)

-vicarious learning for the group

-the way it has always been done

-target is often 'peacefully' portrayed as a necessary: sacrifice, and receptor for- ritualised malice and labelling

-us versus them, from birth, rationale

-vindictive aiming at outer-group members the most popular form of passively aggressive, or actively aggressive, release

-envy regarding individualistic: thinking, intellectualisations, coping, and activities

-promoted to affect individual moral judgement

-endeavours to impact individual political thought, and judgement

-pro-utopianism leanings translate to control falsified as localised, or public, ownership and, in the case of a designated target- control.

<u>*JEALOUSY and PROJECTED BLAME:*</u>

-jealousy of: difference (dovetails with the following category)

-(and frustration) in not being able to infiltrate the target's inner thoughts, reasons for their behaviors and actions, nor their historical, day to day, or their future decision-making

-projected blame: externalization of rejected cognitions, emotions, desires and plans onto a victim/ the prey

-undertakes many forms of psychological, verbal, and sometimes physical abuse

-examples include: within domestic violence situations, or against high-performing employees

-sabotage of the victim may occur fuelled by hostile feelings and dysfunctional cognitions

-as with many other forms of abusive labelling, social comparison is usually primary.

<u>*DIFFERENCE:*</u>

-the victim is typically misperceived and misunderstood

-initial labelling takes hold, as a result

-difference in looks, cultural background, and historical conformity, further the proof and justification (for such actions)

-satisfaction enhances one's (perpetrator's) own perceived attributes

-bullies to the point of reducing the target to group thinking.

PROJECTED ANGER and SELF-HATRED:

-perpetrators' narcissistic core is utilised at all costs

-day to day, and life-long, anger regarding one's own injustices

-an easy individual target is chosen to focus upon

-self-hatred: inferiority complex, and feelings of worthlessness integrated with projected anger from the self-loathing individual onto an often unsuspecting innocent

-inherent criticism of oneself becomes extreme and contemptuous criticism of another.

<u>*INCENTIVISED HATRED:*</u>

-rewards: higher social status within a group

45

-achieves gaining new members

-creates a focal point to emphasise group indoctrination and leader domination, and confirmation that the group's way is the right way

-hatred as credo.

REJECTION of the PAST:

Expanded upon in previous pages, this category cannot be surpassed. It involves primary egoistic overtones and underlying characteristics, which predispose the perpetrating individual/s to life-long execution of labelling, defamation, and victimisation:

-recognition of the target's vulnerability, or lifestyles, by perpetrator's own previous life experiences

-perpetrated via denial of one's own failings and sensitivities

-social cost passed on via labelling of another

-stereotyping and stigmatization transferred from past victim to new victim.

STUPIDITY:

-individual idiots, with non-allegiance/non-membership with groups, perpetrating for the 'play by play' thrill, of a perceived game

-thereby, happy to be photographed during their perpetrations, or respond with verbal calumniation when the target verbally defends themselves

-unthinking, or of low intelligence level

-used as a release from society's burdens by burdening another

-trend-based

-often enthused by social media, localised word of mouth, and resultant creation of enclaves.

<u>**CAMARADERIE (synonymous with childhood) SCHOOLYARD BEHAVIORS:**</u>

-old school allegiances die hard

-recreation of old schoolyard bullying tactics is at its core

-key words (only known to individuals in the 'clique') are used, along with gestures, actions to initiate bullying, labelling, and defamatory statements

-identity-less individuals who seek to develop cliques for hate, vengeance, and malice

-militant thinking

-misuse of the concept of solidarity

-old boys', or girls', club mentality

-the ties that bind never can be broken as long as the use of victimisation is present

-synonymous with religious cultism.

<u>**The OPIATE of SOCIAL MEDIA:**</u>

Not all persons become addicted to, governed by, obsessed with, or determine their values from, social media. However, many do (the opiate of social media is used as an example only).

Topics for further discussion:

-social media and its evils

-social media indoctrination

-social media and individual to group acceptance

-continuity of labelling, slandering and libel/continuous re-affirmation of tweets, likes, ideologies, and chosen targets.

ADDICTIVE VILIFICATION and vengeance:

-satiation of anger

-unending cycle of retaliation

-embracing of base instincts, portrayed via animalistic overtones

-attempts at catharsis

-creating suffering to misperceived restoration of societal equilibrium

-psychophysiological needs (emotional arousal) met

-mistaking calculative manoevres for displays of intelligence and creativity

-militant cognitions and planning.

SEEKING FAME, ADORATION, and (high) SOCIAL STATUS (acceptance):

-to be noticed by a majority, or powerful minority

-wannabe actors or actresses

-surplanting of misappropriated feelings of love, acceptance

-compensating for low self-esteem

-insatiable desire for compliments, even through notorious behaviors

-constant need for adrenaline rush, addicted to dramatic situations

-abandonment issues

-histrionic, borderline, narcissistic, or dependant, personality disorder

-rebelling for no apparent reason

-toxic

-dramaturgy as lifestyle and by way of relating to others.

POLITICO-SOCIAL APPARATUS:

-divisiveness

-power splitting

-stigmatization

-hegemonic framing

-response, reverse, mutual, or counter,- labelling

-re-affirmation of social identity.

<u>*EMPTINESS and NON-IDENTITY:*</u>

"..functions on a pre-guilt moral phase. The focus is on: escaping penalty/ consequences and seeking benefits for their individual actions and words (whether good or bad, as a result)" (3)

-absorption of personality traits of individuals, and group identities

-ever-changing purported values, ideas, and actions

-minimal to no sense of self

-constant change in social roles

-chameleon like

-inappropriate personal boundaries

-co-dependant.

AGGREGATED ACCEPTANCE:

-can be in the form of:

   -social media,

   -cultism,

   -new group formation

-minimal to nil social organization, or skills

-group interdependence slowly grows by denigration of an outside target individual

-alterations to perceptions

-changes to value system

-ritualised, or orientation based, proving of capacity to victimise

-connection develops via timely interactions

-social reciprocity occurs when the perpetrator is determined to have successfully undertaken labelling and targetting.

SARCOPHAGUS of FEAR (created and maintained for the target):

-entrapment makes the heart grow fonder for even more entrapment (hostage-taking) of the target

-no behavior, thought, word or action is correct in the eyes of the self-designated beholders

-the rules change from day to day

-the ultimate aim is fear-mongering

-ownership of the prey is a given

-the target is perceived as an animal to be ridiculed, taunted and abused

-perpetrators' empathy and feelings of responsibility are completely absent

-fear-mongering to the point of annihilation is the ultimate aim.

STREET-SMARTS and PROTECTIVE MEASURES:

-not necessarily gang-related

-although not always the case, the street smart person may present themeselves as from the 'wrong side of the tracks', experienced with crime and/or employ fascist/alienating behaviors towards labelled and defamed victims

-high situational awareness, and thus capacity for depth of understanding of incorrect, hurtful, and damaging, behaviors toward others

-adaptable to differing forms of targetting others

-pragmatic, determined, and survival oriented characteristics ensure relentless pursuit.

-been a behavior from birth, including how to socially relate to others

-socialist community behaviors, as:

    -blessed,

    -infiltrated,

    -inculcated, and

    -culturally adherent

-blind belief on a different scale to religiosity

-indoctrination (from birth, life-long) via literature, paintings, drawings, and local historical writings

-misappropriated empathy

-allegiance to family background teachings

-empowered teaching as an elder (respect, power, status, involved)

-expected general repetition of beliefs, words, and actions

-familial identity (and identification with for instance, socialist ideals) equals identity as grandchild, son, daughter, etc.

BATTLE in the REALM of COMPETITION:

-a perpetrator's psychological reframing of their own lack of/diminished self-identity

-everything is okay as long as it is perceived or presented as a competition, an act, a joke or as a purpose for a cause

-easier recruitment of malicious minded individuals when the concept of competition is introduced (alibi)

-one-upmanship inter-group the norm, to see who can prey upon the most aggressively

-code words, communicating through bodily gestures, controlling, shouting, screaming, and pontificating, varying points of view for reaction and to gain the marked individual's compliance

-savage strategic planners

-step by step approaches to victimization

-treats the victim similarly to marketing of a product.

<u>*HABITUAL UNDERTAKINGS, per friends, social groups, societal contacts:*</u>

-promotion of the concept of enduring camaraderie

-labelling fuelled by kinship

-celebration of the bonds of friendships

-misplaced, addictive concepts of social cohesiveness

-bullying the norm, as a form of social interactivity

-'group think' mentality

-xenophobia justified

-bullying of different targets considered synonymous with sport.

<u>PROFESSIONALS, STUDENTS and OTHER CATEGORIES</u>

Persecutory labelling is identified as:

-idealism personified

-indoctrinated thought

-personal dislike

-wrong assumptions

-self-appointed veterans of a cause

-students identifying as professionals and mentors (before their time)

-students and expectations of conformity

-a class is not just a class, it is a social system, with adherence to self-determined (by powerful in the group) social norms, cognitions and actions paramount for acceptance

-dignity and respect are given contingent on the above adherence to social norms

-bullying and labelling are an accepted part in the case of their social system being
 perceptually threatened in any way

-fun and enjoyment is derived only from celebrating the social order within the class

-collectivist thinking is the only avenue to productive learning

-individual opinions are quashed and sacrificed for the sake of the common good

-cultural differences and historical barriers are ignored, foregoing understanding of
 individual differences to maintain askewed social order

-uprisings, disrespect toward non-compliant educators, and anarchical undertakings are all
 part of celebrating the collectivist approach.

<u>FRUSTRATION, ANGST, MISUNDERSTANDING</u>

Contemptuous stereotyping involves:

-desire for reaching an askewed version of self-actualisation

-misunderstood level of moral stages of development

-only successful form of self-satisfaction

-drive toward greater self-esteem

-lack of co-operation as doctrine

-narcissism

-nihilism

-machiavellianism

-psychopathy

-guilt is always externalised.

<u>HEALTHCARE and PATIENTS</u>

-example of patient labelling, in healthcare: inability to provide diagnosis, clinical response: referral of patient to a psychiatrist

Labelling patients can occur due to, healthcare treaters':

-frustration,

-anger,

-being over-worked,

-incompletion of work (unionised),

-rejection of patient due to region,

-perverse incentivisations,

-anti-certain clients (insurance based, culturally based, clinically based).

-resultant effects: mislabelling (in written report format), misdiagnosis
(or refusal to diagnose efficiently)

-specific instance in healthcare: factitious disorder, and associated labelling

-failure to diagnose as a root cause of the medical problem results- in at best- delayed diagnosis, at worst- an assumption (which then becomes of diagnostic equivalence) that it is all 'in one's head' (patient's)

-where there is a suspicion of a patient lying, overstating clinical problems, or imagining symptoms, the doctor may directly state that the patient needs to be referred for psychiatric help.

In many countries, this can predispose the clinician to legal ramafications down the track:

-in many situations, there is indeed a clinical medical condition, and the delay in diagnosis
 and treatment, can cause unnecessary suffering (and sometimes, worse)

 -Where there exists a complexity, beyond the fact of misdiagnosis, failure to diagnose, or
  delayed diagnosis, a combined example is useful. The doctor makes decisions based on
  the following:
  "presentation of signs and symptoms of illness that do not conform to an identifiable
  medical condition or mental disorder increases the likelihood of the presence of a
  factitious disorder" (4).

However, they must also take into account: "the diagnosis of factitious
disorder does not exclude the presence of a true medical condition.." (4).

<table>
<tr><td>-healthcare: patients' costs of treaters' exasperation</td></tr>
</table>

<table>
<tr><td>-aggressive measures not expected in the realm of clinical medical

practice</td></tr>
</table>

<table>
<tr><td>-rejection of patient, and assurance that they will not return, based on

several factors (and more, as mentioned above)</td></tr>
</table>

ALTERNATIVELY, and formulaically:

<table>
<tr><td>

Failure to diagnose--> Direct impacts (coverage, Healthcare professional

self-soothing mechanisms)--> Psychological labelling--> missing Red flags-->

Human error in Patient treatment-->Cover ups--> Differential coding--> Insurance

impacts

</td></tr>
</table>

That is:

-Failure to diagnose: personal coverage; and Healthcare professional self-soothing can lead to the incorrect labels: psychiatric; and psycho-somatic with concomitant- blacklisting; de-prioritising; assumption that patient is lying; assumption that the patient is stupid; use of power-disempowerment dynamics; and treater based healthcare threats.

ETHICAL HEALTHCARE

Healthcare workers, regardless of their profession, status, and work environment ideally seek to embrace the following necessary qualities and concepts:

-accountability

-efficiency

-patient safety and quality

-values, and beliefs, including moral principles involved in healthcare choices, clinical decision-making, actions, and diagnoses

----

-Beauchamp and Childress: autonomy, non-maleficence, beneficence, and justice (5)

-although considered (in some quarters) as controversial, as it involves perceived moral obligation, the 4 principles are, specifically:

autonomy

-negative duties: avoidance of constraints which control the decision making by patients

-positive duties: treatment with respect in disclosing information to the patient

non-maleficence

-'first do no harm': as in avoidance of undertaking things which are unnecessary

-please see page 77 for a definition of maleficence (in the context of effects on healthcare staff when around toxic colleagues)

beneficence

-a physician's (for example) obligation to act ethically and in the best interests of their patients

justice

-treatment which is fair and appropriate

-provision of equal treatment (sans prejudice or discrimination) for every patient

----

Ethical treatment provided by healthcare professionals also involve:

-quality of care (provided at all times)

-access to care improvements

-ongoing improvements to healthcare workforce

-informed consent (gained from patients, clients)

-patient confidentiality (maintained in all relevant circumstances)

-healthy human factors in healthcare workforce and workplaces

-honesty

-dignity

-respect

-integrity

-empathy

-(where mandated/recommended) open disclosure with patients, caregivers.

Furthermore, for the healthcare provider struggling to combat maltreatment within their workplace, the following applies:

Definition of maleficence in healthcare:

"The malefic bully threatens harm and causes intentional harm. They are regularly termed 'evil'. He/she is a risk to patient safety; purposefully and constantly endanger patients and colleagues as a core part of their clinical reasoning, judgement, practice, and personal beliefs. The colleague is known as one to avoid- at all costs. This is naturally not doable if you are required to work directly with them, in the same environment, clinic, or team. Most, including supervisors, fear the malefic individual. Thus, typically, they escape reprimand and suspension for their wrongdoings." (2)

etc. : etcetera

e.g./eg : example

U.S.A: United States of America

1/ What is the definition of 'defamation'?

2/ Name the 2 main types of defamation.

3/ Describe some of the impacts of defamation.

4/ Which 3 categories can be relevant in seeking damages regarding defamation?

5/ Provide 2 examples of defamation.

6/ How can defamation relate to healthcare?

7/ Explain possible impacts of defamation upon patients.

8/ What is 'SLAPP'?

9/ Name 3 reasons for SLAPP threats.

10/ Describe a situation (of which you have heard) which has involved
defamatory comments or statements, within the healthcare environment.

11/ In the case of becoming aware of corruption, would you have issues with
reporting it?

12/ Provide an example of defamation and its effects upon patient safety.

13/ Name 1 type of 'alternative dispute resolution'.

14/ What is the law which covers deceased persons' relatives?

15/ Name 4 factors possibly involved in worker's compensation processes.

16/ What can become an issue of legality for employers in relation to
defamation?

17/ Name 5 individual perpetrator types most likely to defame.

18/ Describe 'slander'.

19/ How can slander affect healthcare environments?

20/ Describe the factors involved in slander.

21/ Which type of defamation is considered a permanent form of communication?

22/ Name 2 impacts of libel.

23/ Provide an example of libel within healthcare environments.

24/ What is 'libel per se'?

25/ What is involved in a 'john doe' libel suit?

26/ Explain the 'how' and 'why' of the enjoyment of labelling.

27/ What is the definition of 'schadenfreude'?

28/ Name 5 methods of furthering another's misery.

29/ What are 3 reasons for deriving eroticised pleasure in labelling and targetting?

30/ Which 4 components of 'rejection from society' are the most common?

31/ Describe the concept of deviance in relation to labelling.

32/ Provide an understanding of 'rehabilitation to normal'.

33/ Give 2 examples of 'perverse incentivisations' regarding invested allegiance of labelling and targetting perpetrations.

34/ Please add to this description of corrupted religiosity: 'deride... humiliate'.

35/ How can schadenfreude related to the former question category?

36/ Though not isolated to corrupted religiosity, which forms of historical personal experience may be reasons for labelling and targetting of an individual or 'out-group'?

37/ Do political movements sometimes play a part? If so, how?

38/ Which lifestyle differences can be 'fair game'?

39/ Describe 2 types of socialism?

40/ Have you encountered any types of socialism in your day to day, or healthcare work, experiences?

41/ What is the 'norm' in deviant socialist thinking?

42/ Describe 1 difference between socialism and socialistic behaviors.

43/ What is meant by 'individualism is the anti...'?

44/ How can 'peaceful' portrayal of a target be undertaken?

45/ Which kind of blame involves externalization of a labelling and targetting perpetrator's emotions and desires?

46/ What is primary in many forms of abusive labelling?

47/ Name 2 factors involved in targetting because of difference.

48/ What accompanies 'self-loathing' as part of perpetration?

49/ What is meant by 'credo'? Have you encountered such in your personal life?

50/ What is typically transferred from past victim to new victim?

51/ Please define factors involved in the category of 'stupidity'.

52/ Name 3 elements involved in perpetrating on the basis of camaraderie.

53/ Complete this sentence 'the ties that bind…'.

54/ What is meant by the 'opiate of social media'?

55/ Do you agree with the common statement of 'social media and its evils'? If so, in which ways?

56/ When one embraces animalistic overtones as a basis for targetting and labelling, what actually is one doing?

57/ Which type of cognition and planning is used for vengeance type perpetrations?

58/ Describe 5 factors of seeking fame and adoration via labelling.

59/ In which category does 'hegemonic framing' fit?

60/ In which phase of moral development would some targetting perpetrators be categorised?

61/ In your opinion, what is meant by 'chameleon like'?

62/ How can group interdependence grow?

63/ What is determined when a perpetrator has successfully undertaken targetting and labelling?

64/ 'Fear-mongering' is part of the sarcophagus of fear. Which other methods exist?

65/ How do street-smart individuals often present themselves?

66/ In relation to question 65, what is their level of situational awareness?

67/ Which do you believe is most significant in the category 'what grandma told me'?

68/ Which type of perpetrator are often savage strategic planners?

69/ What accompanies the 'bonds of friendship'?

70/ Describe persecutory labelling and students' expectations of conformity.

71/ Explain what is involved in contemptuous stereotyping.

72/ What is your comprehension of 'machiavellianism'?

73/ Please complete the following: 'labelling patients can occur due to, healthcare treaters'...

74/ Which example is provided in failure to diagnose in healthcare?

75/ Detail the 4 main ethical principles.

76/ Quality of care is important in ethical treatment provided within healthcare, which other elements do you believe are also necessary?

77/ What is your opinion of mandated and/or recommended 'open disclosure' with patients, carers/ caregivers?

78/ Provide a description regarding collegial maltreatment of a healthcare worker.

REFERENCES

(1) M.D. Tophus, Victims of Crime: Introduction to Forensic Challenges in Healthcare. Germany: Hilphma Publications: 2022.

(2) M.D. Tophus, The A to Z of Workplace Bullying: For the Healthcare Professional and Beyond. Germany: Hilphma Publications: 2022.

(3) M.D. Tophus, The Unfortunate Healthcare Treater, The Hapless Healthcare Therapist: Narcissistic and Borderline Personality Disorder clients. The Grit. Germany: Hilphma Publications: 2022, p.50

(4) American Psychiatric Association (2022), Diagnostic and Statistical Manual of Mental Disorders, 5 th ed Text Revision: DSM-5-TR. Washington, D.C.: American Psychiatric Association Publishing, pp. 369-370.

(5) Beauchamp, T.L. & Childress, J.F. (2019), Principles of biomedical ethics (8th Ed.). NY: Oxford University Press

113

www.ingramcontent.com/pod-product-compliance
Lightning Source LLC
Chambersburg PA
CBHW070902260726
48661CB00004B/1550